4⁰⁰

MW00436390

PSYCHIC EYE BOOK SHOP
Commercial Center
Las Vegas, Nev. 89104

Max Freedom Long
(1890-1971)

MANA

OR

VITAL FORCE

BY

Max Freedom Long

Selections from

Huna Research Bulletins

HUNA RESEARCH, INC.
126 Camellia Drive
Cape Girardeau, MO 63701

Selections from *Huna Research Bulletins* on **MANA**

by Max Freedom Long

6th Revised Edition

June, 1981

Copyright 1981 by Huna Research, Inc.

ISBN 0-910764-04-2

OTHER BOOKS BY MAX FREEDOM LONG

Secret Science Behind Miracles (1948, 1954)
Secret Science at Work (1953)
Growing into Light (1955)
Self Suggestion (1958
Psychometric Analysis (1959)
Huna Code in Religions (1965)

Introduction to Huna (1948, 1975)
Recovering the Ancient Magic (1936, 1970)
Tarot Card Symbology (1960, 1972)
How Everything Was Made (1967), o.p.

CONTENTS

P r e f a c e

In 1945 interest in Huna was already spreading as result of Max Freedom Long's first book, *Recovering e Ancient Magic* (1936), which had been out of print most from the beginning. The only available source that time was MFL's "Huna pamphlet." Instructional terial on the practical use of the Huna system was eded, as more and more people became interested in e ancient teachings.

To fill that need, Max Freedom Long began a series lessons, which quickly grew into the full-sized book, *e Secret Science at Work* (1953). This book contains e complete text of the third of those original lessons, ich appeared in 1949. Several pertinent sections on na from MFL's earlier bulletins have been added to ke the study more useful. The text is also included Lesson 4 in the course on Huna entitled, *LETTERS ON VA: A Course in the Fundamentals of Huna Psychology*.

Original references to "HUNA, the pamphlet" have en changed to correspond to its current reprinted mat as a paperback book, *Introduction to Huna*, by Freedom Long (Esoteric Publications, 1975). To the erences to SSBM (*The Secret Science Behind Miracles*) ave added sections from SSAW (*The Secret Science at k*), GIL (*Growing into Light*) and HCIR (*The Huna Code Religions*).

It is hoped that you will find this study as eresting and valuable as other Huna students have ing the past thirty-six years.

Dr. E. Otha Wingo, Director
HUNA RESEARCH, INC.

e, 1981

Readings

Introduction to Huna, pp. 17-19 and 31-32.

The Secret Science Behind Miracles, pp. 97-99;
    p. 352 (center); pp. 389-390. Also run
    through the book and check mentions of
    Mana and its many uses in the various cases
    discussed.

The Secret Science at Work, Chapter VI: "Mana
    and the Surcharge of Man," pp. 77-83; see
    also references in the index.

Growing into Light, Chapter 15: "The Breath of
    Life," pp. 161-168.

Huna Code in Religions, Chapter 7: "The *HA* Prayer
    Rite as the First Great Mystery," pp. 75-91.

Letter of Contact

Dear Friend and Huna Research Associate:

A number of years ago I knew a man who was very successful in buying and selling ranches and farms. One day I asked him how he came to succeed so well. After some hesitation, he told me that as a young man he had discovered that certain people were "a power with God in prayer," and that he had helped these people and in return they had prayed that he be given guidance in his buying and selling. For twenty years he had been the sole support of a color-ed woman and her family. She had seldom failed to "pray him through," but, and this is what I am get-ting at, on the rare times when she did fail, she explained simply, "De Lowd jest waren't to home to me fo' some prayers, some times."

When I told this story to my father, he laughed and remarked, "Those times must have been the ones when Monty had driven too hard a bargain."

So, with your attempts to use the Huna prayer-action methods, it should be remembered that in all we do we are part of the world family, and anything that we ask that might take advantage of another mem-ber of the family, will probably get us no opening of the door of heaven when we knock.

One of the great difficulties is to get past the old dog-eat-dog rule of life of the animal world in which "survival of the fittest" keeps the life strains up to par. As savage peoples, we humans live much by that law. It is the law of the subconscious spirit in us even now, and we must watch to see that we train our low-self "George" so that he can grow into the more kindly and helpful ways of life that make the conscious mind or middle self quite different.

Small children are animated by the low self and must be trained from the will to "grab" to the will to "give". Some of us "never grow up," at least in this respect, and most of us have to examine our lives daily to see that we have not fallen back into childish selfishness without realizing it.

In your approach to Huna you will, perhaps for the first time, come to see clearly that you, as a being of three closely related spirits (low, middle and High) must try to remain aware of the obligatic on each of these three levels of life represented b three levels of consciousness.

Most of us in our approach to religion have fallen overboard with a resounding splash into the lovely and enchantingly intoxicating sea of High Se ideals, in which we see ourselves giving ALL and as ing NOTHING. Soon we find that this will not work practice because something has to be kept for one's own use. Even the wearers of the yellow robe must keep what is dropped into their begging bowls if th are to eat. So we drop a little of the idealism an wade out to shallower and safer waters where we giv a tenth of our ALL and get along better. Soon we find that even kindliness sometimes will fail us. W find that someone who is actuated by the law of "Gr must be met and dealt with--and in his own coin. the moment we fight and struggle in a mud puddle, f from our intoxicating sea of ideals. And, in this level of living, which we cannot avoid because we live in an animal body, we may win out or may be be en badly.

A good Huna Research Associate will get on bet than most because he knows that he must function an grow on and through and into all three levels. He knows each level for what it is, and he does not ma the mistake that has been so universal--the mistake trying to carry the ideals of one level into the on above or below. He will SERVE as best he can, and with great and impersonal love. He will be kind an helpful. These attitudes cover the two upper level of living. For the lower level, he will fight as hard as he can, be it with germs or fire or flood o thief--but while doing it, he will keep the door op to HELP.

--MFL (1949)

ACCUMULATING AND USING THE MANA SURCHARGE

In the psycho-religions, both ancient and modern (with the exception of Huna) there is little to be found that gives us a clear idea of the POWER that turns the wheels of life or that moves the machinery of prayer.

In Christianity there is vague reference to the *virtue* that left Jesus when the hem of his robe was touched and a healing resulted. In prayer the POWER was ascribed to God (*"Thine be the Power"*). No conscious use of vital force was clearly indicated as a part of the prayer-action.

In the beliefs of India, much is said of *prana* (which may have been an idea drawn from a source similar to that from which Huna was drawn). Prana was held up as a tool of value in the early Theosophical writings, but later was denied the devotee on the ground that, to use it for healing prevented the "working out of karmic debt through suffering." The shining example of a force of this kind was found in the legendary "serpent force" supposedly rising at the base of the spine in response to certain exercises (performed by the purified initiate), and rising in spirals along the spine until the top of the head was reached. There the force caused the "open consciousness" and one "saw God." Much has been added to the older idea of centers along the spine and in the head, so that now the nerve centers and glands have been pointed out as the parts used in this process of seeing out from the body as from a window let into heaven itself. I spent several months trying to get proof of these mechanisms when young and a member of the T.S. I also tried for some years to find any person who gave evidence of having learned to arouse and use this force, but without success. While one denies nothing, one can safely conclude that the *use* of the specialized forces recognized in Indian lore is hardly to be expected by the average student.

The simpler theory is that consciousness (as a Creative First Source) creates FORCE, and from force (possibly when limited by time-space) is derived MATTER. Our men of science are slowly deciding that all matter is a form of force, and, if the move in this direction continues, the conclusion will probably be reached that force is a product of some form of consciousness.

In Huna the very practical kahunas decided, it would seem, that our middle-consciousness self is incapable of understanding the higher forms of consciousness, so needs waste no time over anything but the forces which can be handled on the lower levels—the low and middle vibrations or voltages of mana.

To the kahuna, *life* was consciousness plus mana plus the invisible aka substance. When the three were in and around a living body, the material of the body also became *alive*, but it died if the consciousness-mana-aka was withdrawn.

Mana alone was not considered *life*. It was on the FORCE used by the entity. (Three entities, of course, and so three manas). The Hawaiian word for "life" is *ola*. This translates, from the roots *"o"* and *"la"*: "belonging to the light." The word "light" (as of the daytime) symbolized human consciousness in contrast with the higher Light of consciousness symbolizing the High Self. (*La* is daylight, and *La-a* is the Higher "Light", the ordinary translation being "Sacred".) As we see, in this symbolic unit of the ancient Huna secret, *life* is made up of consciousness and something else that *springs from it:* the vital force. In passing, it may be well to note that the kahunas seemed to have a word for the rather neglected matter of reincarnation. Like many other matters which they seemed to consid beyond the ability of the conscious mind to grasp, or beyond the powers of the subconscious self to measure in terms of the senses, they made up a simple word for the fact, and were at no pains to hide in its roots a secret meaning. The word seems to be *o-la-ho-nua*, which is now translated as "thoroughly, completely, or altogether." The roots give us "life," plus "preceding or going before." Breaking down *ho-nua* to *ho* (for *hoo*, the causative) and *nua*, we have "to cause dust to fly in traveling," which is a picturesque way of pointing to their symbol of the "path" which was the symbol of growth through the many levels of consciousness as well as of the aka thread and the contact through it with the High Self. (As I now understand it.)

The union of the ideas of *life* and *mana*, in the minds of the kahunas, is to be seen in the word *ola-ola*, which is a doubling of the word for "life." This compound does *not* translate "more life;" it translates "to make a gurgling sound with water, as in pouring," and there we have the familiar symbol of "water" for mana. Surely all these many words which tie in to weave back and forth to tell the same story, over and over, in the same symbols, are not to be tossed aside as of no significance by students working in this field.

In the presentation of these materials to you, I pointed out the belief that vital force or mana must be provided by the lower man for the use of the higher to whom he prayed, so that the High Self would have sufficient earthy force to affect the dense and earthy level of life.

This idea is unique in the psycho-religions, as I have explained. It is, I incline to believe, the largest third of the lost key to instant healing. The other two-thirds are made up of the thought-forms of the prayer, and the part played by the High Selves in building the thought-forms into a reality in the future of the one making the prayer. (Check the word for this use of the thought-forms, *hoana*, on the bottom of page 395 of our text, SSBM. The root *ano* means "a form," and the roots give us the real meaning of "to cause a form"--the thought as the form of the thing prayed for--which the external or common translation is, "to reverence in the highest degree," which is the meaning stressing the devotional side of contact with the High Self. Another translation is, "to set apart"--as the thought-forms are "set apart" or "consecrated" by giving them to the High Self. Another is, "to change the appearance or form of a thing," which is the basic work done by the High Self in changing the crystallized future for us to something more in keeping with our desires.)

In Lessons I and II, we have considered at great length the first step of the prayer-action, that of deciding what is wanted. (See particularly SSAW, Chapter VII, "Making the Prayer of Thought-Form Clusters," pp. 97-114, and Chapter X, "Summary of the Huna Prayer Method," pp. 127-136.) We have touched on the careful making of the picture of the desired condition as a means of making the proper thought-forms to be used as molds into which the future is cast in some mysterious way by the High Self when supplied with the proper amount of mana.

Roughly speaking, the theory is that the more mana we supply consciously for the work, the quicker the High Self can answer our prayer. (Provided the thought-forms are properly made and the work is not held up by a guilt fixation.)

In our experimental work as Huna Research Associates, we are testing this general theory in a number of direct as well as oblique ways. We never forget for a moment that we cannot be sure of our theories until we have made them work repeatedly under proper test conditions.

Once the thought-forms were made, the surcharge of vital force was accumulated to have on hand after the contact was made along the aka thread

with the High Self and the thought-forms presented
as the idea behind the action. (Also, as we will
consider at length later on in the Lessons, there
was a preliminary cleansing of guilts or guilt fixa-
tions--called *ka-la,* "to cleanse" or "restore the
light.")

THE ACCUMULATION OF A SURCHARGE OF MANA

This part of the making of the prayer-action
consists of:

1. Deciding what you will do with the surcharge. (In making a prayer to send with a flow
of mana to the High Self, you use the extra supply of mana in a different way than when you place
your hands on someone and give them the mana as a
part of "low magic" healing. If you plan only to
practice accumulating a surcharge, you will plan
to make a test to see how well you are charged,
or you may be content to do no more than enjoy the
benefits of having your normal supply of vital
force brought up to par, or above that. One HRA
recently practiced accumulating extra mana each
time he looked at a bit of paper pinned on his
wall. He also recharged when driving, each time
he was held up by a stop light. The result was
the ability to work much longer hours with much
less fatigue than before. There are other uses
which will be discussed later on in connection
with other parts of the experimental work.)

2. Giving the order to the low self to do the
actual work of accumulating the surcharge.

3. Making use of some physical stimulus to get
the low self to go to work, or, possibly, to help
in the accumulation. (Exercises or breathing or
postures, for example).

Fortunately, we do not have to know just what
the low or subconscious self does when it accumu-

lates vital force at our command. On the other hand
unfortunately, we cannot be entirely sure that the
low self has carried out our orders. For this reason a series of tests has been worked out to check
up. The electronic machines used by some manipula-
tive physicians will show on their dials the difference between the normal and the augmented charge.
The use of a simple pendulum is coming into the fore
Or the magnetic pull demonstrated so well by Baron
Ferson provides a test where several people are prac
ticing as a group.

THE PENDULUM TEST

The Pendulum Test is perhaps the simplest for
the beginner. A round button the size of a small
marble may be suspended from a thread six inches
long and used. A small pottery marble may be glued
to a thread. Or, one of the best I have found in
the home-made line is constructed by taking a piece
of sealing wax about 3/4 of an inch long and fasten-
ing to one end of it a piece of light string or a
bit of heavy thread. The string is easily fastened
to the end of the piece of sealing wax. Heat one
end of the wax over a flame, taking care not to set
it on fire, and when it has softened, use the end o
a match to push the end of the string or thread dow
into the softened wax. Then, with the fingers,
squeeze the wax up around the string to hold it
firmly. As soon as it cools, your pendulum is read
to test your charge.

The first step is to determine your normal
charge or charge of the moment. Hold the string
between thumb and finger-tips about three inches
from the wax or button "bob". Keep your elbow
against your side to steady your arm, and hold your
free hand, palm upward, under the "bob" at a distance of about half an inch.

If you are of the usual sensitivity in the
matter of pendulums, your pendule will soon begin

to swing in a circle or back and forth, according to
your personal vibration (supposedly). As soon as the
movement gets a fair start, begin to count. Keep
counting the swings until the pendulum stops or
almost stops.

Fifty gyrations above the hand before the surcharge is accumulated is a usual thing with many
people. After the effort has been made to accumulate
the surcharge, the number of swings may increase to
from eighty to three hundred. My personal average
is about fifty and when charged for prayer work about
one hundred eighty.

Many theories have been advanced to account for
the fact that a pendulum will swing in different ways
to indicate different things, but the theories are
not important to the student at this point. However,
it may be noted that the ancient art of "dowsing" to
find water and for various purposes has a large lit-
erature of its own and is in itself a fascinating
study. The low self may be responsible for the
swinging of the pendulum and it may also be actuated
in its work by information had through the High
Self. Dr. Oscar Brunler, who has made a long study
of such matters, believes that it is the High Self
that works through the low to tell the dowser where
water is to be found when the pendulum is swung over
a map to locate the exact place to dig. There is
increasing evidence that we can train the low self
to get information concerning the already set or
crystallized future from the High Self and to give
us "Yes" and "No" answers to our questions concerning the near future. HRA Edgar W. Block used this
method in his experimentation and was able to pre-
dict correctly the outcome of six consecutive basket-
ball games. He also named the correct score of one
game in advance, it being 38 to 32.

If you are unacquainted with the pendulum work,
and should you wish to try your hand at asking questions and expecting the low self to get the answers
from the High Self (if relating to the future), there

is nothing against doing so.   Try asking questions,
the answer to which you know, and observe what the
pendulum does.   Once you come to know what it does
for "Yes" and what for "No", you can begin practice
that may eventually give you a fine tool with which
to pry into the secrets of both low and High selves.
However, take my advice and do not bet on the horses
after testing the scratch sheet with the pendule.
If you have ever been well convinced that gambling
is not good, your low self will probably do all in
its power to prevent a win.   (See SSAW, Chapter II,
"Getting Acquainted with the Low Self," pp. 14-32.)

THE FERSON METHOD

The method of accumulating the "Universal Life
Force," which was taught by Baron Eugene Ferson and
which I have described in SSBM, is one that includes
a physical stimulus and an affirmation as well as
a self-command.   It works very well for most people,
whether we believe that the force we call "mana"
comes from the utilization of the food materials in
our own blood stream, or is drawn from some outside
reservoir of force in air or ether.

To use the Ferson method of accumulating a surcharge of force, stand with feet very wide apart an
arms extended level with the shoulder, palms anglin
slightly upward, if that is an easy and natural pos
tion for you (not important).   When this position i
taken, hold it and say aloud, "The universal life
force (or just Mana) is flowing into me now....I
feel it."   Repeat this about four times, slowly, an
with a pause of about twenty seconds between repeti
tions.   Expect to accumulate a surcharge, and expec
to feel a prickling in the palms of your hands or i
your wrists, to indicate the building up of the
extra charge.

It is surprising how quickly the low self lear
to respond and collect a surcharge in answer to our
desire.   Hardly anyone fails to get results.   Some

get amazing results almost from the first, and are
so surcharged that their arms and hands seem stiff-
ened, or they may have a "floating" sensation.
(Gravity seems sometimes overcome by such a surcharge. Dr. Hereward Carrington's experiments with
the young man standing on scales and doing breathing exercises makes good reading. There are many
other SPR reports on similar "levitations.") [See
SSBM, Chapter III, for other examples of such experiments. Also, variations of the Ferson method are
described in SSAW, pp. 76ff.]

THE MAGNETIC PULL TEST

The magnetic pull test for a surcharge of
mana is made in the following way:

1. Accumulate as large a surplus of mana as you
can.
2. Have a friend who has not a surcharge stand
in front of you, back to you, hands hanging at sides
and relaxed. The distance between you should be such
that when you lift your arms you can lay your hands
lightly on your friend's shoulders.
3. Lay your hands on your friend's shoulders
lightly and then slowly withdraw them, pulling them
after you as you take a very slow step backwards.
4. If you have a large surcharge and your
friend has a small, normal charge, your friend should
feel a distinct pull, as of magnet-like force, from
your outstretched and slowly retreating hands. If
the pull is great, it may be necessary to catch the
friend to keep him from fall backwards. There will
be no feeling of pull on your hands no matter how
strongly they "pull". Individuals vary greatly in
their response to this pulling test, and you may
find that in a group of a dozen people, one or two
will be far more sensitive than the others, and so,
much better to use in making the test. Animals may
also be used, as explained in SSBM in telling of my
tests in which a small dog was pulled backwards

several times despite his efforts to resist.

BREATH AND MANA

Breath and its part in accumulating a surcharg
is not yet fully understood, but seems to have a
peculiar significance. My personal guess is that t
extra mana is manufactured by the low self by burni
foods stored in the body for that purpose. Such ox
dation is going on constantly, but when we exercise
strenuously, we always breathe more heavily and we
become hot from the excessive burning of blood suga
to produce the vital force that enables us to do th
work of exercizing. *(Note: This "guess" was confir
and it was also found that mana is breathed in from
the atmosphere along with oxygen. Cf. the works of
Wilhelm Reich on "orgone energy." EOW.)*

In the usual course of exercise or physical
work, only a small surplus of mana is made and whil
very large amounts may be made in the course of a
few minutes or of several strenuous hours, it is US
UP as we go along. There lies the difference. In
accumulating a surcharge without exercise, the supply is held instead of being used up in muscular
activity. It is, therefore, there and standing rea
to hand to be used in the prayer-action, or in layi
on hands to treat someone who is ailing.

Breathing, in itself, is a form of exercise.
involves the use of the chest muscles and especiall
the diaphragm, but the production of extra energy b
forced deeper breathing is out of proportion to the
additional muscular exercise. From the yoga practices we have learned that we can take deep breaths
for a minute or two and feel much refreshed and
stimulated. If we hold the command over the low se
to accumulate a large excess of mana and store it i
the body (and the low shadowy body or aka), the ful
benefit will accrue. The act of breathing deeply,
slowly and evenly, will serve as a physical stimulu

to impress the low self that something real is being done (not just imagined), and the additional intake of air will help the physical process of manufacturing mana. (See the excerpt concerning physical stimuli on p. 20 of this book. *The importance of the physical stimulus cannot be emphasized too much!*)

In using the Baron Ferson method, I have found that I begin to take deeper breaths almost at once. The same thing is true when I simply remain as I happen to be, standing, walking or sitting, when I command my "George" to accumulate extra vital force for a prayer-action or other use such as in telepathic contact and telepathic transfer of vital force and healing thought-forms.

"LET GEORGE DO IT!"

"Let George do it!" has laughingly been proposed as the slogan for Huna Research Associates, and it gets across the idea so well that I am constantly referring to the low self or spirit in us as *"George"*.

The conscious mind or middle self-spirit-soul (each of the three selves is a "soul" as well as a spirit in Huna) is a strangely helpless entity. It cannot control the body except through control of "George". It is a guest in the house and is suspended, as it were, between the low and High selves, able to do little for itself, but blessed with its own form of reason and so able to do its share by bossing the job of living, at least on the lower levels of consciousness.

We must constantly keep in mind the fact that in Huna everything depends on our ability to guide and command the low self, once we have decided what is to be done. In the simple fact that we must *"Let George do it!"* lies the secret of why our prayers have been answered so seldom, and why we get such scant results in our use of the more modern "affirmations," "holding the thought," or "decreeing."

Often the people who are simple and uneducated have
much better success with prayers than the highly
educated. This would seem to be because the former
are working better with their low self.

Easy relaxation needs to be learned if one is
to get "George" to obey and to work smoothly and
happily with us. We have to LET GO in order to LET
GEORGE. This is an axiom of modern psychology and
it fits Huna exactly. If you do not believe that
you have to give "George" his head, just try forc-
ing yourself to go to sleep when you go to bed to-
night. You will soon get the idea. All you can do
is to get yourself ready, and then turn the job ove
to "George" and fold your hands.

If, after you have taken all the steps and hav
finished a prayer-action, you will remember that yo
have done little more than set a pattern of the
thing to be done, and have commanded "George" to do
it, you will be entitled to a silver star to glue c
your Huna "Sunday School Attendance Card"! If you
drop off and take forty winks, awakening much refreshed, you are entitled to a gold star. If you
keep fussing at "George" for fear he is not doing
his job--just because you cannot see or hear him at
his work--it will be as bad as digging up the seeds
every day in your garden to tell them to grow.
"George" is like a seed in that respect. Plant hin
and let him alone.

MAPPING THE FUTURE

In beginning your practice it is a good thing
to decide what you want built into your future, anc
write it down! Writing it down is a physical stimulus of value. The written word impresses the low
self, whereas thinking is usually ignored because i
seems to be unreal--just more imaginings or day
dreams. One maps the future in this way. But, goc
as this is, the best way in the world to prevent

your map from materializing is to show it to a doubt-
ing friend and have him scoff at it. "George" is so
sensitive to adverse suggestions! Follow the old
adage: *Dare* to make your map, *Do* by taking steps to
get it built into your future, and *Keep Silent* about
it unless you have a friend who is more convinced of
the efficacy of Huna in your hands than you are.
This is where you "go into your closet to pray in
secret." After some twenty centuries we know why.

I have watched the working out of prayer-actions
for some months, and can now give it as my opinion
that a beginner will do well to take up the things
in his map one at a time. If you have to make a half-
dozen prayer-actions to cover the half-dozen items,
that is all well and good. Make them. Space your
prayer-actions a day apart if you can, but at least
an hour apart.

Because I am one who believes greatly in Huna
and in the ability of the average HRA to learn to
use much of it, I have been privileged to see a number of maps and to help by making a prayer-action on
them. Many a map has read something like this:

> *"I wish my sight and digestion healed."*
> *"I wish my income doubled."*
> *"I wish my son to pass his examinations."*
> *"I wish to be able to use Huna to heal*
> *others."*
> *"I wish to be able to do worthwhile service*
> *for the world."*

This type of map is good. It is reasonable.
It is one asking for things not difficult to picture and to believe possible to attain with the help
of the High Self.

THE THOUGHT-FORM MOLD

In making the thought-form mold into which the
desired future is to be cast, figuratively speaking
(we cannot know the exact way in which the High

Selves use these molds), we are confronted by the problem of keeping our thought-forms clear-cut and uncontaminated by doubts, fears, and tag-ends of other ideas. For instance, in the map above, the work of making a good clear mental picture of the eyes restored to normal vision needs to be done wit out at the same time trying to carry beside it, but well separated, the picture of the digestive organs functioning normally. If, in addition, the picture of the normalized eyes and stomach was made to in- clude the doubled income, it would become a slight jumble. Add the other items and the mixture would be anything but clear.

Visualization of the thing desired (one item a a time) should be undertaken long enough before the actual prayer-action to give plenty of practice and plenty of time for a good job.

One may imagine a time in his future (not necessarily a definite time), and begin imagining himself as in that part of the future and with the desired conditions fulfilled. In the above maps on might dwell for several minutes in the future. One is at home as usual, but can see normally. One PROJECTS oneself into that bit of the future and spends some time enjoying and using the restored sight. One looks at things closely, one tells visiting friends how nice it is to see perfectly again. The picture is made as vivid and detailed as possible, thus stressing the idea of the USE of the normal eyes.

We have all made the mistake of thinking that this visualization is something that can be done at once and without practice. As a matter of fact, it has turned out to be as difficult a task as memoriz ing a ten verse poem, perhaps more difficult. With the poem you have nothing to unlearn before you can really make progress.

The thing about the normal-sight visualization that must be forgotten as a preliminary is the FAULTY SIGHT. We have found that it takes practice

and effort to step into a pictured future and begin
seeing normally. We keep dragging along the eye
trouble instead of leaving it behind as we step
through into the future.

It helps mightily to talk confidently, and
aloud, about the new condition which one is building
into the future in this work of making the thought-
form mold. The talking is a *physical stimulus* and
impresses the low self. One holds conversations and
says to an imaginary caller, *"Yes, my sight has been
perfect and normal now for some time, and I know
that it will remain that way. I can see as well as
I ever did. I can read for hours. I thank the High
Self daily for this great blessing, and I thank the
low self for its part in obtaining it."*

DR. BRUNLER'S METHOD

Dr. Brunler, mentioned in connection with the
pendulum, uses the following method of accumulating
a surplus of vital force. He stands facing the
north and rakes the air with his hands, fingers wide
spread, as if using them to pick up vital force from
the air. (Cf. Baron Ferson's method of gathering in
"Universal Life Force"). The hands are lifted above
the head at the full length of the arms, palms facing forward. The arms are kept straight and the
hands brought down in a sweeping circle with the
fingers raking through the air. At the same time
the body is quickly bent far forward so that the
hands can continue making their circular sweep, ending it only when the arms are as far behind one as
they can comfortably be brought. This is repeated
briskly from fifty to sixty times while holding in
mind the command to the low self to accumulate vital
force. As this is good exercise, the breathing auto-
matically quickens.

I have not been able to find an exercise or a
physical stimulus that may have been used by the
kahunas, although their words used to name the steps

in their use of Huna indicate from all angles the b
lief that the surcharge of mana was needed. The us
of a mental picture for a physical stimulus is
strongly indicated in a word which means "to rise ●
like water in a fountain until the water overflows
This method is a favorite of mine. One sits or
stands and begins to breathe more deeply while picturing the mana accumulating in the body, beginning
at the feet and rising until the whole body is progressively filled and there is an overflow at the
top of the head.

The overflow at the top of the head is a very
significant symbol, and I make it a practice of in-
structing my "George" to contact the High Self when
the accumulation is well along. The contact made,
I instruct (and desire) "George" to send a flow of
the mana to the High Self along the aka thread of
connection. This is where the water "fountains"
above the head, symbolically, and when the High Self
has accepted the low mana and changed it to its High
Mana (*waiola* or living water, or actual "holy water
not blessed by human priest), a part of it is used
(we suppose) as requested to further its own purposes and help others and perhaps help bring better
world conditions, the other part is returned to us
as the downward fall of the fountain water, the
"rain of blessings" which is requested at the forma
ending of every prayer.

When I feel the work of accumulating the mana
has reached the fountaining stage, I say to "George
"*We are now reaching out and making contact with ou
loving and utterly trustworthy father-mother parent
spirit. We are sending a large part of this extra
mana along to it by way of the aka cord. We offer
as a perfect sacrifice, to be used for the good of
all of us or as may be seen fit.*" I pause here for
about half a minute to relax and "let go and let
George" do the work, then say: "*The flow stops. Th
action is finished. Let the rain of blessings fall
Au-ma-ma (or Amen).*" This is the REAL and effectiv
DEVOTION. It is the ONLY WORSHIP that COUNTS, so w

learn from Huna.

"DIVIDING THE WATERS"

In all of our uses of mana in prayer-actions and in laying on hands, the offering of a part of the mana (*wai-pa*, "to divide the water," to pray) is of great importance. This is the secret behind the libations poured by the ancients before drinking their wine. This is the secret of "Grace Before Meat." It is the secret of all offerings and sacrifices, no matter how far they may have drifted from the original intention of the sages who first discovered the great SECRET in the dim past. We serve the earth and the lower creatures and they feed us. We serve our friends and they serve us in return. We serve the High Selves with the worship of the "Dividing of the Water," and by helping those fellow men about us who are the beloved charges of other High Selves. Serve others in this way, with generosity and kindliness, and you make powerful friends of their guardian Aumakuas. Conversely, injure others and those same powerful guardians may take steps to prevent your continuing in unkindness. Be kind--always.

A DEFINITE ENDING

The formal ending to the prayer-action may be delayed for as much as an hour after we have given "George" his instructions and have repeated our prayer. But the mental and physical relaxation should be continued during this time in order to give the low self time to carry out our instructions. If we begin doing other things and thinking of the affairs of the day, the low self is recalled to take its part in that work, leaving the prayer-action incomplete in all probability.

One first makes the mental picture, clear and

perfect, of the condition which will be presented as a set of thought-forms to the High Self to be used in the rebuilding of the future. Days may be spent on the different items to be used in separate prayer actions.

When the mana surcharge has been accumulated, we hold the command-desire in mind to cause the low self to contact the High Self by activating the aka thread of connection. We then call up as a MEMORY the prepared visual picture of the desired condition. This brings into the focus of consciousness the thought-forms of the condition. We then ask to have the visualized and desired conditions built into the future so that they will soon appear as realities in the present. For example: *"I ask that this condition of normal sight be made into a reality in my future. I will then see perfectly and normally in every way, and I shall continue to see perfectly all my life."* One may describe in careful detail the exact condition imagined in the future, repeating almost word for word three times, with calm force and assurance and confidence in the outcome.

While we are repeating the oral part of the prayer-action, the low self will, when it has learned the work, after some practice, possibly be engaged at the same time in carrying the thought-forms along the aka thread, with the flow of extra mana, to the High Self. Or, it may begin this work only after we have become silent and have relaxed and perhaps said, *"All right, low self, deliver our prayer and the mana to the High Self."*

WHEN CONTACT IS MADE

As a rule, in trying to make contact with the High Self, one feels, at least once (perhaps as a given proof of the completion of the contact) a great thrill of sudden joy which may have a heavy emotional content because the low self (which controls all emotions) is involved. The eyes may fill with tears

of joy. It is an ecstatic condition of which the
mystics of all lands have left their records. It
is very real, quite unmistakable, and greatly re-
warding just of itself. It may be a glimpse of a
higher octave of the love we know on this level--
the higher and more unselfish love.

REPETITION IS USUALLY NECESSARY

Some day, when the practice period is over and
one can be sure each time that the prayer-action is
completely and properly made, a single request for a
desired condition may be enough, and can be allowed
to stand while we wait in full faith and confidence
for the appearance of the desired condition. However, as beginners, we can only keep repeating our
prayer-actions, each time trying to make them more
perfect, until we begin to get results by way of
answers. It takes time. If one begins with simple
things, the answers come more quickly.

I knew an old gentleman, living on borrowed
time, and with one hand tightly clutching the hand
of his Aumakua, who was continually losing his hammer
or tools about his work. Invariably he paused to
pray to be helped to find the lost tool, and I never
saw him fail to find the lost tool shortly. It
appears to be a fact that we are permitted to ask
for almost any small help.

The pendulum may prove to be a great help if
you can get correct "Yes" and "No" answers to questions through it. The low self could tell you
whether it had accumulated a surcharge, whether it
had made contact with the High Self, and so on. This
use of the pendulum is just being investigated as I
write this advice. It may turn out to be a greater
help than is now expected. Remember, always, that
we are taking part in an experimental project.
Invent ways and try them out.   --MFL (1949).

THE IMPORTANCE OF PHYSICAL STIMULI

[From HRA BULLETIN 27, page 8, March 1,]950]

After observing the healing work of "Ted" [a healer not otherwise identified by MFL] for several weeks, I have concluded that it takes more than a great surcharge of mana to do successful healing. He naturally registers a large surcharge, and while laying on hands and repeating the Lord's Prayer, his charge runs up to ten times his high normal, as certified by H. Crozier Leigh, M.D.(cf. his article on page 83 of March-April [1950] number of *Astrology Guide*). HRA Leigh measured patients after treatment by Ted and another natural healer with a similar gift, finding that they retained a surcharge of mana for up to an hour, and that this had excellent healing properties, but that usually the treatments needed to be continued daily where more than a simple thing like a headache was concerned. My present opinion is that Ted is hardly skirting on the High Magic of Huna, and that his work under the low magic could be much bettered by training and practice in making the correct thought-form picture of the healed condition and projecting it on the flow to the patient. So far the part of the physical stimulus has been almost entirely ignored, and so the effectiveness of the healing greatly limited. When the healer fills the patient with mana, little happens unless the patient's unihipili is made very fully and clearly aware of what it is to do with that mana by way of correcting the physical ills. All the rituals of the older churches and of the kahunas were aimed at impressing the low self. It is not enough to lay on hands and repeat the Lord's Prayer. The patient's "George" has usually learned to rattle off that prayer and to expect no result because of the rattling. Its very lack of success with that prayer in the past serves to set up a barrier against help that may be offered at the moment by the High Self.

Prayer is not a "thinking". It is a combination of thinking and a GESTURE or actual physical movement of the low self in the body--a creation of mana and a giving of it.

THE "PERFECT" RITUAL

We should invent a physical ritual so definite that to perform it would take all the concentration of the low self--and thus prevent it from going aimlessly through the action with you while its mind, in its behind-the-scenes department, is really engaged with something entirely different. Preliminary fasting, with sincere efforts to make amends for hurts done others, or to make general amends for lacks and faults--all these are part of the gesture we make to arrive at the beginning of the successful prayer. I know of no way to convince the stubbornly literal low self that it and its man deserves an answer to prayer except by the performance of physical acts--the use of the acts as a physical stimulus. Remember, "Faith without works...." --MFL.

(Note: It may be well to point out that such a perfect ritual for use as a physical stimulus cannot be standardized and published for general use. Some printed meditations and ritualized prayers may be very useful. But the PERFECT ritual will be the one that each person works out for himself--for the particular purpose of a specific prayer-action. EOW.)

* * *

"Where love and strong emotional desire is not felt when a prayer is made, one may be sure that the low self is not doing its part, and that the prayer will be ineffective." --GIL, p. 59.

WHEN THE "MIND" WANDERS...OR

CONTROLLING THE LOW SELF

[From HRA BULLETIN 32, pages 2 & 3, May 15, 1950]

It is the common experience of many HRA's that immediately after sending the mana to the Aumakuas, they find that they tend to fall almost into sleep. The mind wanders and the work becomes dim and mechanical. For this reason, I wish to make the suggestion that after you send your surcharge of mana through the braided cord to the Aumakuas (or through your own low self via the aka cord to the High Self), a pause of about a half-minute be made and *a new charge of mana accumulated.*

If a pause is made and the mana supply is built up again by your favorite method, the sleepiness caused by the lowering of the mana charge will depart, the middle self will again have mana to use in exerting its "will" and there will return a brightness and mental clearness such as is needed in picturing the "world at peace" and the following mental images of the desired conditions.

When the mana level falls below the easy reach of the middle self, figuratively speaking, the low self slips the leash and goes racing off. We are not aware of this unless we have learned to watch for just such things. Ordinarily we find ourselves in a dull state in which we are mechanically going through our prayer rite, speaking aloud or reading the words, but almost unaware of them. We may not become aware for some time that other thoughts have intruded themselves in the back of our minds and their drift is causing that strong pull that is bending our attention away from what we are trying to do.

This is a very important thing to understand. So far as I know, no ancient or modern psycho-

religious system or "teaching" except Huna explains
the fact that the middle self or "conscious-mind"
self is able to control the low self or "subconscious self" ONLY if there is a sufficient charge
of mana or vital force in the aka or body to allow
the middle self to get enough of it to use as "will."

The "will" is nothing hard to understand. It is
low mana taken by the middle self and put to use as
middle mana (*mana-mana*), the purpose of which is to
control the low self. Without such control, the
low self is cast adrift and left to its own devices.
Invariablly it will begin playing with remembered
ideas, and these are what we find drifting through
the back of the mind, becoming more and more clear
until, unless recognized and checked, they fill the
entire mind and crowd out the thoughts we are trying
to think.

The full charge or even the surcharge of mana
is one of the very basic things in prayer of any
kind. Huna has taught us that if the low self and
the middle are to work alertly, purposefully and
effectively together in the act of making a prayer,
there must be enough mana to supply the power for
the thinking processes of each self. Modern psychology does not deal with prayer, but from it we
learn that if the supply of vital force falls to a
low level, the control of the "subconscious" is lost
and we are on the way to possible insanity.

Here is something which I wish very much to
get across to you. It was not stressed in my book,
I fear, but it needs to be understood and kept in
mind as the sum total of the difference between the
prayer that gets an answer and the prayer that does
not. As you know, we are forced to fall back on
comparisons or analogy when we try to understand
anything about how the Aumakua or still higher
beings think or act. This is because the low and
middle selves are unable to use the form of thinking which is used on the next or still higher
levels of conscious being. We use our reason and

go as best we may from the knowable and known, to the unknown.

Following this one and only method (because "revelation" is in such poor repute and so contradictory), we see that:

1. The low self must have mana to live and act

2. The middle self must be able to draw the mana it needs from the low self if it is to use its powers of will and mind or to function effectively in the work it alone can do.

3. Granting the truth of the above, we follow the analogy and decide, as did the kahunas of old, that in its turn the High Self, which is a part of the triune man, must also be able to draw sufficient mana from the low self to be able to perform its work, whatever it may be, effectively.

Where there is no mana, there is no life, and what is of even more importance to us at the moment, there is NO THOUGHT. (The kahunas used the word *mana-o* for "to think". It means literally "something done with mana.") In the word *Au-ma-kua* the root *ma* means "to wilt." Wilting is caused by a lack of water, and water is the symbol of mana. It is plain that the ancient kahunas, when coining the words which describe the things having to do with the "SECRET" or Huna, had no slightest doubt that the third self of the man had to be supplied with mana just as did the middle self. It follows that if the kahunas were able to do a fraction of the things which we know they did do, this piece of knowledge was sufficiently correct in its basics to work. Our task as HRA's is to learn to know what the kahunas knew and, like them, to make it work. The old world is sick-unto-death of things which do NOT work. It has had too much of the speculative and of assertions for which no valid proof can be offered. The accumulation of a surcharge of mana and the sending of part of it to the High Self as we make thought-forms by praying appears to be auto-

matic only when the low self is moved by great emo-
tion. At other times we must take the needed steps
ourselves.   --MFL

* * * * * * * * * *

RECHARGING THE BATTERIES

A VERY IMPORTANT DISCOVERY CONCERNING MANA
[From HRA BULLETIN IX, page 2, May 15, 1949]

It has been well known for many years that work
of a psychic nature often is very exhausting. When
we began our experimental work with Huna, we prompt-
ly ran into the fact that many of us fell asleep in
the midst of our prayer-actions after consciously
sending a flow of vital force to the High Self.
Others felt tired out after the prayer-action was
finished.

I was repeatedly warned by those long experienced in healing (by laying on hands and by the
help of spirits acting as guides and healers, but
drawing vital force from the operator for healing
uses). On the other hand, friends who had always
prayed to the High Selves (or Universal Mind, Christ
Spirit, etc.) had found that they escaped the exhaustion so common to those depending on the other
methods or sources of help.

In our own work with Huna, I, therefore, urged
that we all invoke the aid of the High Selves in all
of our experimental efforts. I think that we have
all done this faithfully, but the exhausting effects
of long treatment were still reported.

A few weeks ago I undertook to explore this
part of the field and find, if possible, the cause
of the tiredness and the remedy. I had concluded

much earlier that the exhaustion was caused by a lowering of the level of the normal charge of vital force (low mana) in the physical body and in its surrounding and interpenetrating shadowy body (*aka kino*). I had seen many hypnotists gradually increase in power and ability, only to become unable to work because of the utter weakness following strenuous use of the hypnotic abilities--as in giving shows, or treating several patients in one day. Dr. Nandor Fodor had pointed out the fact that mediums had to rest about half of the time to regai the lost strength. The danger of insanity was know to be strong progressively as the mana charge was lowered too far by one thing or another. (Mental causes as well as bodily injuries or disease.)

The kahunas symbolized this loss of the normal charge of mana as a "wilting," "fading," or "wearin out." (See Andrews' *Hawaiian-English Dictionary* fo the root meanings of *ma* in the word *mana*.) From other symbolic Huna words which use the word for water (*wai*) as a part of a plural-root word covering this same idea of loss of the normal mana charge, the symbol is that of "underground loss of water by seepage, as from a *kalo* pond."

I should (knowing what I already did) have see the problem so clearly that I could put my finger o the trouble and the remedy at once. But, like so many things in Huna, this was a point not yet cover clearly in modern thinking, and I had been unable t see the forest because of the trees.

Finding that I was becoming increasingly tired by the three and seven o'clock work in which I acte as the center for "braiding the cord" (aka threads) for the Telepathic Mutual Healing Group, I set abou finding a way to test the mana charge in my body, and settled on the use of the pendulum as the simplest and best method.

One evening I took my home-made string and sealing-wax pendulum and made the customary test of my own index charge of mana. It registered the usual fifty-two clockwise gyrations when held over the palm of my left hand. I then made my usual use of the Huna method of accumulating the surcharge of vital force, and as the hour of seven drew near, found that I tested my usual 230+ gyrations. So far so good.

I took up the box of letters which are used in the TMHG work to make the aka thread contacts with those joining in, and held the pendulum over their edges. (They stood on edge in a cardboard box held on my knees.) The pendulum swung rather weakly back and forth across the edges at right angles to them. (As usual.) When the exact hour arrived the pendulum increased its swing and reacted with about a third longer swing. This kept up while the High Selves were being invoked and the combined mana flows united in the "braided cord" and sent as an offering to the High Selves (*Poe Aumakua*). As I began sending out the usual telepathic images to those taking part (to act as a check on contact, etc.), the pendulum motion slowed down but kept swinging in the same direction. When the images had been sent at 7:04, the pendulum stopped swinging almost entirely while we made our mental pictures (thought-forms) of the conditions to be built into our futures. (And while I took up the letters one by one in my left hand and called clearly to mind the images I had made previous to the evening in question.)

At 7:07 the pendulum again began to swing strongly, in the same direction, seeming to indicate the flow of mana in through the aka threads to the High Selves, and carrying with it the thought forms of the prayer-actions. The swing remained strong until after 7:08, when the work was ended by the usual, "*Let the rain of blessings fall!*" (return flow of the High Mana in some form). "*A-ma-ma.*" At that moment the pendulum changed quickly and swung at right angles to its former direction, ALONG the edges of the letters instead of across them. The movement lasted about half a minute, during which time I felt a strong tingling (the usual thing for me).

I set the letters aside and found that I was suddenly very tired and sleepy. It was with an effort that I took up the pendulum instead of taking a short nap as had lately become my custom. I held the pendulum over my left palm and it *registered only 19 small gyrations!*

I realized at once that the eight minutes of intensive work had used up most of my normal charge of mana as well as the surcharge with which I had started. It was very clear that the mana had *actually been sent out and used up.*

Pulling myself together with an effort, I fought off the sag and inertia of mind and forced myself to begin breathing deeply and accumulating a surcharge of vital force. My low self was very slow to respond, but in about half a minute the feeling of "swimming" laxness of mind began to go. By the end of a full minute the normal condition of easy control over the body and mind was definitely on the way back. I became mentally refreshed and alert, and soon began to feel wide awake and ready to plunge into my work. I took up the pendulum again and tested my charge. The reading was 89 gyrations. In less than four minutes I had recharged myself and was more rested than at other recent times when I had napped for as long as fifteen minutes.

I COUNT THIS ONE OF OUR GREATEST STEPS TOWARD INSIGHT, and I offer thanks and congratulations to several HRA's who have helped to bring the problem to a focus so that we could get the answer. HRA Russell P. Schofield has been especially helpful. He carried on a series of experiments in recharging himself many times a day while at his exhausting mental-physical work, and found that he could recharge swiftly at any time, all day long, and that he could work double the hours with less weariness.

I cannot too strongly recommend making it a practice to pause and recharge at any time when there is a mental sag or dullness. In fact, any mental condition that is undesirable or out of the normal run of things should be benefited. If one is overtaken by timidity or indecision, or the feeling of not being able to "face it" or "go another step," here is the magical remedy. Breathe deeper and more strongly. Build up a surcharge. You will then find that the sun shines again and all prospects become normal. We no longer have to "drag" through our days and our work. We can charge up and get "George" back under control in a matter of minutes because it makes the conscious self strong and positive.

In treating ourselves for health conditions, I feel certain that the hourly recharging with vital force will be of the greatest importance. I suggest that when a surcharge is accumulated, the low self should be instructed to work with and for us to carry an "offering" of vital force to the High Self. Speak softly and say something like this: *"Loving Parental Spirits, I reach out to you now and send along the aka thread this offering of vital force. Accept it to use for your own purposes and to help the world and me.* (A pause here of a few seconds to let the low self do the work.) *Let the rain of blessings fall. Amen."* Then, while refreshed and alert and strengthened (or cleansed by the return flow of High Mana), call up your picture of yourself as normal in health and prosperous, happy and filled with the joy of Service. This will be cumulative in its effect.

I am indebted to HRA Wing Anderson for finding for me one of the key things in the *OAHSPE* bible. Here is the first clear and definite statement found in any of the revealed writings (insofar as I know) to verify the conclusions reached--that the High Selves NEED THE VITAL FORCE WHICH WE CAN SUPPLY--

that we MUST GIVE it to them if they are to be
easily able to do the many things that affect this
lower level of life and help us. It is a verification of the findings made in our study of the kahunas' words for "altar, sacrifice and worship." In
Report Bulletin III (reporting on the TMHG work) this
deeply significant matter was explained in detail
and for the first time.

The *OAHSPE* verification is to be found on page
396, Chapter XX, passage 6ff. In these passages
there is described a war on the higher planes of being. In it the "ashars" (Guardian Angles or the Huna
High Selves) were attacked with great force by evil
forces. Here is the central point:

> *"Again the threatening adversaries stormed,*
> *and wondered whilst they stormed, that one*
> *alone stood so boldly in face of such great*
> *odds and flew not away at once. And every*
> *ashar laid his hand on the sleeping mortal*
> *in his charge, for by this his power was*
> *multiplied a thousand fold."*

It stands to reason that our High Selves, being
spirits without dense physical bodies other than the
one shared by the three selves of the man, need the
force of this denser level of living to work in the
denser materials, as in healing. We see that at
seances the spirits MUST have vital force to use for
all their work in producing apports, transportations
and materializations. They take it from the medium
and the circle, often leaving them all exhausted.

While this idea that we must "nourish the gods
if they are to nourish us," is not new in India, it
has been misunderstood in other lands and their religions. We have thought that the "gods" had all
the power and that we must beg a part of it for ourselves. In Christianity we pray, *"Thine be the*
Power, and the Glory...." In modern terms we speak
of drawing the "Universal Life Force" from some
"Universal Source" which is under the control of

"Universal Mind." It begins to stand out with startling clarity that the low (subconscious or *unihipili*) self and the physical body are the SOURCES for the force that is used on all three levels of life in which the three selves operate. (No matter where the force comes from originally, whether it be from sunlight reaching the earth or from other basic first-sendings, the original force supposedly used by some form of consciousness to create our universe is beyond our reach of mind, so need not be considered seriously.)

The whole effort aimed at the testing and restoration to understanding use of the ancient "True Light" of the kahunas, would be well worthwhile even if this discovery of the secret behind the use of the mana in working with the High Selves were the only one made. Fortunately, we are making one discovery after another. And each step brings us that much closer to the ultimate goal--to come to know the High Selves and to work hand in hand with them, and under their Guidance.

* * * * * * * * * *

MANA--A LIVING FORCE

The strange nature of the manas needs to be taken into consideration in all studies of healing methods out front on the pioneer fringe of things. We cannot stress too often the thing known to the kahunas--that mana is a *living force* and that it can and will obey the commands given it. These commands are first given to the low self by the middle self. The low self, who controls the low mana, will collect a surcharge of the force, will concentrate it in any part of the body desired, or, for instance, after concentrating a surcharge in the right hand, will cause it to flow from the hand into a part of one's own or another's body needing healing.
[From HRA BULLETIN 70, January 15, 1952, p. 8]

* * * * * * * * * *

GUARDING THE MANA

[From HRA BULLETIN 53, April 15, 1951, page 2]

GUARD YOUR MANA.   In a recent letter the question was asked: "Why is it necessary to break contact with the High Self and finish the prayer abruptly as we do? I like to keep the contact and commune with the High Self--sometimes going to sleep that way." HRA Major O. B. Gabriel, who is an experienced healer and who works at times with Harry Edwards in England, wrote in the magazine *RELIGIONS*:

> *"But the passing of human vitality--*
> *sometimes called Magnetic healing--is*
> *only one, the lesser in fact, of two*
> *types. The greater is the transmitting*
> *of a Power from* without *the human frame.*
> *The difference is easily discerned in*
> *practice, for whereas the Magnetic healer*
> *gets depleted, to the point of exhaustion*
> *if he continues too long, the Spiritual*
> *healer ends up better than he began."*

In our work we make our prayers when in direct contact via the aka thread, with the Aumakua. We send the mana as our offering. That is a basic part of the ritual and we have to perform that act for ourselves, not depend on the Aumakua to do it. Each self must do the part assigned to it, and in this case the low and middle selves are responsible. When the prayer-action is over, it has been found by experience that, for some reason or other, it is also necessary to invite the return flow of mana-- mana raised to the High-Self level of power and purity which can heal and bless. The kahunas asked: *"Let the rain of blessings fall."* We must do the same. It seems to be a part of the act of opening the door to the help of the Aumakuas so we may have the aid they are forbidden to give unless their presence is recognized and their aid requested. Always, without exception, we should make this

formal ending to prayer if an offering of mana is
sent to the High Selves. That ending made, we may
then resume contact and happily commune--rest in
happiness of the warm nearness, dearness and love of
the Utterly Trustworthy Parental Spirits. One may
also visualize the mana rising as in a fountain in
the body, fountaining above to the Aumakua and re-
turning to you as water to the fountain bowl. This
establishes a complete circuit and one can then pray
or treat for a long period of time without being
depleted. I use this method in the TMHG (Telepathic
Mutual Healing Group) periods here at the Study.

                                            --MFL.

                  * * * * * * * * * *

POTENTIZED MANA

[From HRA BULLETIN 72, February 15, 1952]

POTENTIZED MANA (in the Homeopathic sense) may
well be the secret of what we postulate to be the
"High Mana" or *Mana Loa* of the original Huna system.
As I have said in my book, SSBM, it is evident that
the life force--mana or basic vital force--is used
in seance work when ectoplasm is taken from the living and used to fill the aka molds of entities who
materialize. This seems to demand a form of force
that is "living" in as much as it can be controlled
by the mental action of spirits (they having no
mechanical means of control such as coils and vacuum
tubes for such uses). We know of no non-living
force which can be so controlled, as, say, ordinary
electricity. It follows that if mana is taken from
the living at a seance and used to produce materializations or apports, the amounts of mana must be
rather small, otherwise the medium and sitters in
the circle would be far more depleted than they are.
This leads to the conclusion that the mana must be
"potentized" in some way so that a small amount of
it can do spectacular things. In my book I suggest-

ed the idea of stepping up the vibration of the force much as we do in handling electricity. I hav been taken to task for this comparison repeatedly, and will be for suggesting "potentizing" as a comparative process. But, be that as it may, it appears quite evident that *something* is done to chang the vital force so that it can perform in a way not seen under ordinary circumstances. Perhaps we may eventually, thanks to pendulums and related semi-psychic extensions of our measuring mechanisms, learn exactly how low mana becomes High Mana and is used to break down non-normal parts in the body and rebuild them as normal or "healed." In any event, so far as I can learn, Huna offers at this time the one and only simple, clear and logical explanation of what happens in this poorly lighted corner of the field in which we labor as HRA's. (p. 2)

PRAYER AND MANA EXHAUSTION have often gone together for many of us in our Huna prayer-action experiments and in the TMHG as well as when trying to heal individuals with physical contact. The pendulum test of the normal charge of mana also is good for the surcharge, and for the condition of charge after mana has been sent along the aka threa to the Aumakua or Great Company of Aumakuas where the flow may possibly be divided many times and in some manner "potentized" greatly for use on that level of being as well as on the physical level.

Sleep is the natural reaction to a lack of mana....However, it is my opinion that if one successfully establishes a circular or up-and-back flow of mana, with the Aumakuas, and is careful to ask for the return flow as in the words, *Let the RAIN of blessings fall,"* the mana, as the pure water-mana of "rain" will not only be returned but will be watched for by the low self and accepted. Just a little "potentized" or High Mana, according to our present theory, will vivify one amazingly as well as act to heal and otherwise aid the physical or mental man. (p. 4)   --MFL.

NECESSITY OF MANA CONFIRMED

[From *Huna Vistas* No. 19, March, 1961, pp. 1-4]

THERE IS MOST EXCITING RESEARCH NEWS to report in this issue of the H.V. It is that at last I have come upon confirmation of the fact that in Huna there was the belief that mana had to be sent with a prayer to enable the High Self or the "Great Company of High Selves" to have the needed earthy force to work on their level to bring about the desired conditions specified in the prayer. Also, there is confirmation of the belief that the prayer had to be strongly built in terms of thought-form picturings.

AS MOST OF YOU KNOW from reading my books and bulletins, much of the recovery of the ancient Huna lore was accomplished by studying the root meanings of one word after another of the compounded words used by the kahunas to name elements in their beliefs and practices. In addition to the meanings of the roots, there were symbol words to be understood, as, for example, the word "water," standing for *mana* of any kind.

WHILE THE SECRET CODE OF THE KAHUNAS was gradually broken in this manner, even to breaking the code as used in the New Testament and early Yoga writings, there was often nothing to be found in the very scant written material from the kahunas to show that the conclusions reached from studies of the code were correct.

NOW, AT LAST WE HAVE DIRECT CONFIRMATION on one of the strangest and most unique beliefs and practices in Huna. At an early period in the research work, it was realized that there were certain things to be found in other religions which seemed to resemble the things turned up through the word studies of Huna. More than that, there were great similarities between the phenomena of Psychic Science and the findings of modern Psychology. For instance, the Huna words in which the root *aka* appears, were not understood in their inner or code meaning until comparisons were made to our knowledge of the ectoplasm of the seance room. Hinduism, via the priceless studies of the early Theosophists, gave the clue to the three *aka* or "shadowy" bodies of the three "selves" of Huna. The *prana* of Yoga led to the understanding of the basic force or *mana* of Huna, and eventually to the three uses made by the three selves of the basic mana, these uses being IDENTIFIED by the different USES, as in the case of the mana when used by the High Self to cause instan or slow changes in physical matter, as in miraculou healing. (For convenience we think of the mana as having three "voltages" or speeds of vibration as in the case of radiant energies such as seen in light or radio braodcasting.)

OF ALL THE DIFFICULT-TO-ACCEPT BELIEFS found i Huna, the one of the three selves or spirits has caused the most objection. We had all been taught that a man had ONE SOUL, and to split it into three separate souls or "selves" caused rejection on the part of many Christians. In Yoga there were traces of the earlier Huna belief to be found, particularl in the "high" and "low" parts of the "self" as mentioned in earlier writings. The Theosophists, in giving us their findings after endless sorting of conflicting and tangled beliefs current in India, stopped short of giving us the concept of three independent (although closely associated) selves. In stead, they confused the "bodies" with the characte istics of the recognized facets of the accepted ONE self. (This statement will bring me arguments from some of the HRA's who still prefer Theosophical cor clusions as against those I feel are of the early and original Huna.)

THE SECOND MOST DIFFICULT thing from Huna to accept, especially by the HRA's of Christian backgrounding, has been the need to send mana along the

aka cord to the High Self as a part of the prayer.
We were taught to stand up and say our prayer, and
that was the whole of it. And, because some prayers,
even those uttered silently at a moment of danger or
desperation, were certainly heard and answered, it
was thought that the Huna preparation of the prayer
ahead of its delivery, and with the gift of mana,
could not be necessary. "God is all-powerful,"
reads the dogma, and all prayers were addressed to
God, with the Christian addition of the "This we
ask in the name of Jesus as our intercessor." (Jesus
being the Huna High Self introduced at some early
date into Christianity by kahunas using their secret
code to veil their inner teachings.) The outer rite
of offering sacrifices in many religions replaced
offering mana. We cannot be certain that the mana
of sacrificed animals or birds did not serve some
real purpose. But in Christianity the blood sacrifice vanished, as it did in the inner or uncontaminated Huna found in Polynesia. However, the only
open hint that mana might be offered with the prayer
is found in the non-Huna part of the New Testament,
supposedly given by Paul. He advised: "...that ye
present your bodies a *living* sacrifice, holy, accep-
table unto God, which is your reasonable service"
(Romans 12:1).

THE BASIC IDEA OF SACRIFICE IN HUNA has been
worked out through a study of the roots and word-
symbols of words used by the kahunas (Hawaiian).
Mo-hai or just *hai*, means "to sacrifice." *Ha'i*
gives the meaning of "to break," and suggests the
breaking in two of a thing so that half of it can
be used as a sacrifice. Jesus "took bread and broke
it" in the coded mystery of the "Last Supper" and
his blessing and passing of the wine takes us back
to the pouring of an offering or "oblation" to the
gods, so common in olden days, but having behind it
the great Huna mystery of "dividing the waters"--
that is, sharing the water or mana with the High
Self. The *ha* root in the word for "sacrifice" warns
one who is initiated to watch for the heavy breathing

(*ha*) by which a surcharge of mana is created to serv
as the "living" or "life" sacrifice to the High Sel
along the aka cord of connection. The kahunas had
words for all the forms of sacrificial offerings
known to the early Hebrews. They are listed in the
old Hawaiian dictionary (Andrews) over which I have
pored so many hours, and in the list is the compoun
word *mo-hai-hoo-mana*, BUT WITH NO MEANING GIVEN FOR
IT.   This word is left out in the modern Hawaiian
dictionary. Apparently some learned kahuna who
helped the first missionaries in Hawaii to make a
dictionary of the Hawaiian language, gave the word
but, as it was part and parcel of the Huna "Secret,
refused to say what it meant. We have only to
translate it to see what it meant. The translation
is: *"To sacrifice by making mana."* The symbol word
idea of "to make mana" is code for accumulating a
good surcharge of mana and sending it to the High
Self. *Hoo-mana* also means "to worship." The roots
appear time and time again in the words connected
with the use of Huna and the mechanics of worship,
cleansing and prayer. It is all there before the
student, BUT one does not find writing in which som
initiate into Huna says DEFINITELY what the secret
meaning may have been.

NOW WE COME TO OUR DISCOVERED "PEARL OF GREAT
PRICE." In the last issue of Huna Vistas I spoke o
a small book which someone had sent to me. The
title of it was *He Sent Leanness* and it is by Davic
Head. I quoted a prayer from it, then dropped the
short review, only to discover, a few days later,
when continuing my reading, that there was somethir
priceless to us on pages 51 and 52. Let me quote:

> There have always been those in the Church
> who have been most at home with the doctrine
> of Creation that man is made in the image of
> God, however much that image is distorted.
> Primitive man has a deep sense of awe and
> worship, far deeper than that found in many
> Christian congregations today. Dr. Nels Ferre

begins his book, *Strengthening the Spiritual Life*, by quoting Mother Alice Kahokuoluna of Hawaii:

> "Before the missionaries came, my people used to sit outside their temples for a long time meditating and preparing themselves before entering. Then they would virtually creep to the altar to offer their petition and afterwards would again sit a long time outside, this time to *'breathe life'* into their prayers. The Christians, when they came, just got up, uttered a few sentences, said Amen and were done. For that reason my people called them *haolis*, 'without breath,' or 'those who failed to breathe life into their prayers.'"

THERE WE HAVE IT! *Ha* is the Huna symbol of accumulating mana and sending it to the High Self (or Selves). *Ole*, the second root of the word means "without." In the dictionaries the meaning of *ha-ole* is given simply as "a foreigner." Not a word is said of the origin of the word, and one may well suspect the early makers of the dictionary of purposefully avoiding the true and apparent meaning of the word as given above.

MOTHER ALICE KAHOKUOLUNA ("Star in the Heavens Above") was pastor of the first Protestant church built on the Island of Molokai (where the famous leper settlement was). The church was named "The Church of the Healing Spring" (Siloama) after the Pool of Siloam at Jerusalem, where, according to the Bible story, an angel came to trouble the waters betimes, and those who entered the pool at such a time were healed. The church still stands, even if more modern churches came later at another spot in the settlement. Rev. Alice Kahokuoluna was called "Mother" by those she served in illness as well as in the matter of their religious needs. Half-Hawaiian and well educated in our Eastern seminaries, she now flashes like a bright star for us, also, in our long efforts to learn the great secrets of Huna and, which is very important to our work, give us direct and impressive proof that we are right in at least one basic conclusion concerning the Huna beliefs and practices....The very fact that we have had from her one such direct proof of correct insight allows us to believe that, on the whole, conclusions reached through similar studies of Huna words and symbols are fairly reliable.

THE MEDITATION AND PREPARATION before approaching the "holy place" (High Self) is described in the code with *hoo-aka* (the root *hoo* is the causative pre fix meaning "to make" or "to cause") which means to "make very clear and properly understood." This is serious business because one must be very careful to weigh all elements in the proposed prayer for a change in conditions, then picture the desired condition in careful and clear detail. That can be called Step One.

STEP TWO is *hoo-iha-iha:* "to cause the drawing tight of a rope," the Huna symbol of activating the aka cord that connects the low self with the High Self. A secondary meaning is "to be intent," and this well describes the state of mind before making the actual prayer.

STEP THREE is *pu-le,* "to pray." The root *pu* means "to come forth, as words from the mouth," also to try to talk while holding WATER in the mouth, which would make no sense to us did we not know that water means mana, and that the mana as well as the words of the prayer must come forth to go to the High Self. The root *le* is found in *le-le,* "to leap or fly upward," symbol of the passing along the aka cord to the High Self of the thought-form picture of the desired changed condition, as well as of the upward flowing of mana. The word *lele-huna* symbolize the upward flying of fine particles of something, or of the fine drops of water in mist. *Huna,* as the code root in the full word, shows us that the thought-forms (which are symbolized as tiny and invisible particles) are to be accompanied by mana, the latter indicated in the meaning of the "water" composing the mist or "fine rain."

STEP FOUR begins as the prayer is presented at the symbolic altar (sent to the High Place or Aumakua). One may then settle down to the work of sending a sufficient amount of mana to allow the High Self to break down the old future before it can arrive, and replace it with the new and desirable future condition. The word *hoo-mana* has the dictionary meaning of "to cause superhuman power" and "to cause one to have regal authority." The mana is transformed by the High Self so that it can be used to make the desired changes. We might say that by giving the mana to the High Self we give it regal authority, and in so doing we say, "Not my will but thine be done," giving the Aumakua full authority to decide upon the good of granting or denying the answer to the prayer.

STEP FIVE comes after much or little time has been spent accumulating and sending mana. For a miracle of instant healing in which a broken bone is dematerialized to be rematerialized unbroken in the mold of the uninjured aka of the bone, we suppose much mana is needed, while for the giving of intuitional guidance, the need might be small. In any case we learn from Rev. Alice Kahokuoluna that a considerable time might be spent AFTER delivering the prayer to *"breathe life into it."* From other words and roots we gather that a difficult answer may be made less difficult by daily repetition of the prayer-action and the renewal of the supply of mana. Prayers were repeated three times word for word very often.   --MFL.